I0555083

Phoenix
The Crash, Burn & Rise

BREE SPRUAL

Copyright © 2024 Bree Sprual

All rights reserved.

ISBN: 979-8-218-42865-5

DEDICATION

To my daughter, who saved me in ways that I didn't know that I needed saving. And, to my friends and family who sat and grew with me in the dirt until I was ready to bloom again.

CONTENTS

FOREWORD

Phoenix is personal; A book of poems that take you on a journey through the shadows and brings you into the light, with the rising Phoenix. This forward is not enough space or words to express the level of growth and self-love that oozes out of Bree's pores now. I have watched her literally claw her way Out of the Trenches. From being unsure of whether to live or not & not knowing what each day is going to hold...to watching her CHOOSE joy and healing for herself and living in her authentic truth. This book is emotional. It requires reflection, grit, and understanding of self. But it's also prideful, loving, warm, and true. Thank you, Bree, for committing to yourself, and helping others along the way. I love you, always.

- Jaymee Vee, Author of "*Black Girls Don't Commit*"

THE CRASH & BURN

You give love and take it away.
When I need you, you never stay.
So instead, I write the words I could never say.

If I sing you every love song and write you all the pretty words…
Will you stay?

I used to love so freely,
Now I hold it hostage.
Healing a broken heart,
Has left me so exhausted.

What is the standard of love for someone who has never seen it?

The truth about loving after heartache is that it's scary.
What if I trip over your pretty words and fall head over heels for you?
The broken parts that I pieced together so carefully may be too shattered
to mend again.

The silence is too loud.

She's angry with me.

She wants to be heard,

To be loved.

So, I turn the music up.

I ignore her.

I'm afraid of what she has to say.

-The girl in the mirror

You were all I wanted.

And you punished me for it.

A love dealer,

Giving just enough to get me hooked before you withheld.

And watched me wither from withdrawal.

Just give me one more hit.

There was once a time that I thought the world of you.

Now I just add you to a list of people that I wish I never knew.

I grieve the girl I was before them more than I grieve their absence.

I found you when you were broken. I fixed you just for you to break me in return.

I picked the wrong men. I picked the men who I could see my own brokenness in. And as my heart ached for them, I wanted to help heal them in a way that I wished someone would care enough to heal me. The problem is that I ended up giving parts of myself to make them whole again, and then I would leave even more empty.

I became hard to protect myself. Please don't coax the soft girl out of me just to damage her more.

I have a lover's heart and a cynic's mind. I won't believe a word you say yet my heart leaps with every syllable that leaves your lips.

The thing about my love is that it is circumstantial. You will either bask in it or burn in it.

You broke the girl I was and then went looking for someone whole.

I painted you beautiful.
Softened your edges with dainty strokes,
Adding light into your darkness.
I removed your flaws,
And accentuated your strengths.
I used the most exquisite colors in my palette to paint the memory of you as
someone worth being missed.
I painted you beautiful.

What a mess we've made.
What a monster we've created.
The tangle web we've weaved,
Leaves love unsatiated.
Starved of affection,
Gasping to breathe.
One day I'll gain the strength to finally leave

You tell me you don't want to hurt me,

As I sit on the floor fumbling with the pieces of me you intentionally broke.

I thought the world of you.

But you didn't think of me at all.

Not with her,

And certainly not in Houston.

You thought you saw the hurt in the aftermath of the pain that you caused. But the truth is, that was me being strong. If you saw it raw, if you felt the way it gripped my hurt and shocked my core…. There'd be no way you would be able to face me. You'd realize that "sorry" could never fix what you broke.

You wanted me until you had me. Then I fell for you and the hard exterior cracked and faded away. I was laid bare, and you grew bored. Did my rawness offend you? You told me you loved me but decided my love wasn't what you wanted anymore. How carelessly you seemed to throw that word around.

When the rest of the world is quiet and asleep,
I let my mind wonder to what we could've been.
If you were a better person or I was a weaker woman.

We grew up in a time where "what happens in the house stays in the house." But if these walls could talk, they'd tell you the horrors they've seen. If people knew you, the real you, then that small town in Texas would no longer be impressed by your money. They'd see the darkness that holds your soul and know that is where the true monsters live.

When you battled your demons, I held you down.

When I battled mine, you dragged me down.

We are not the same.

Maybe one day we will look back on this time as a beautiful moment of vulnerability. But that is not today. For now, we will bask in the light when it shines on us and try not to drown in the storms.

Nothing is linear.

Not pain,

Nor happiness.

Not healing,

Nor grief.

What you heal from today,

Could kill you tomorrow.

I accepted the love that I was taught was normal. The hurt was always a part of the packaged deal.

My body is a costume that I wear in public. I put it on and go to work. I say the right things, laugh, make jokes. People say, "You're so put together." But at night, I peel myself out of the costume. I lay in bed too tired to think. How exhausting it is to bring this character to life daily.

There is a black hole where your heart used to be and that is not your fault. But you allowed me to swim in your love and drown in the absence of it- and that I do blame you for. So here it'll end without a sequel and now you know why I don't fall in love with people.

I thought depression was a constant state of despair but its not. Its drowning day after day. Finally making it to the top and taking a deep breath of air only to be drug back under. Depression is a battle against the tide.

If we only have tonight
Love me long & hold me tight.
We'll pretend tomorrow won't ever come,
& your promises won't end with the morning sun
Whisper things we know aren't true,
To make me fall more in love with you.
Let's fool ourselves that this is right,
Even if it's just tonight.

I can never pinpoint what comes first,
You pleading to be let in
Or me clinging for you to stay.
In the end it always ends up this way

Whose fault is it really? Yours for leaving? Or mine for pushing you away anytime you got too close. You'd have thought I would have learned long ago not to make a game of "tug of war" out of love.

Kisses are not contracts,
Love does not mean needing.
Together doesn't mean "wholeness" just as single doesn't mean "lonely."
Promises are not binding,
And there is a subtle difference between holding a hand and chaining a heart.
You'd think by now I'd remember these things.

We go around and around.
At some point, we need to acknowledge that we are fire and gasoline.
A spark between us and we could light the world on fire.
So why are we so confused that we keep getting burned?

If I was a flower in your care I'd wither.
Your hateful words spewing venom leaving me un-watered.
My petals crushed under the heavy burden of your expectations.
Yet somehow, you 'd still stop to gawk at the flowers in bloom.
You fix your lips to start complaining about the destruction you created.

I've fallen in love with the same guy since I was 16,
They've just gone by different names.
It's time to acknowledge that maybe I'm the one whose toxicity has damaged
my perception of love.
To keep choosing a love that takes and never replenishes.
Why do I keep accepting a love that leaves me feeling lonely,
Even when I'm not alone?

You loved me because I was strong but loving you made me weak. Then you pulled away because the idea of me was better than the reality. Because the chase is always better than the capture. You want access to the light parts of me without acknowledging my shadows.

People say if you're depressed you need to speak up.
But they mean that in theory- not execution.
Because nothing makes people more uncomfortable than you showing your
demons to them.
For God's sake, you're a woman!
You're supposed to keep it all together.

Nobody has been crueler to me than I have been to myself. Why is it so hard to foster love with the one I lay in bed with every night?

I really can't be angry.
In fact, I just feel bad.
Cause one day you'll wake up,
And miss just what you had.
When the booze runs out,
And the girls forget your name.
One day you'll wake up,
And you'll want to stop the games.
You'll miss my obnoxious laugh,
And you'll probably try to call.
But by then I won't love you,
Not a little, not at all.
So go ahead and get wasted,
Take a girl home every night.
But when the party is over,
Who will love you right?

It's a tight walker's rope,
The line between healing others and hurting yourself.
Lean too far to either side and you'll fall,
Consumed, wholly.

Fragile petals fall,
Love's ghostly ruins,
Heartbreak's silent call

You were always trouble,
I knew it from the start.
But I chose to trust you,
So I broke my own damn heart.
I really can't be mad.
They told me you were cruel.
Whispered all your lies,
And played me like a fool.

In the quiet depths where shadows play,
A heart once whole, now frayed and gray.
Love's gentle touch, now turned to dust,
As whispers fade, in silence trust.
Each beat a echo of what was before,
Now hollowed out, an open sore.
Memories dance in the empty hall,
Echoes of laughter, now silent call.
A shattered dream, a broken vow,
Tears that fall like raindrops now.
In the wreckage of what used to be,
Lies the remnants of you and me.
Yet in the darkness, a flicker of light,
A glimmer of hope in the endless night.
For from the ashes, a phoenix will rise,
With wings of strength, it takes to the skies.
Heartbreak, though painful, will not define,
For in its wake, new beginnings shine.
So let the tears fall, let the pain subside,
For in the healing, love will abide.

Broken promises & broken bones
Growing up in broken homes
Anxiety & constant fear
Abuse that made me want to disappear.
Instead, I bloomed & won't look back,
A flower that grew from a sidewalk crack.

THE RISE

Slowly but surely, day by day,
The pain recedes, the hurt goes way
Healing is not a destination,
But a journey of self-restoration.
And though the path may twist and bend,
In the end, you'll always win.

Even though I've been hurt many times before, I still dream of a version of myself that is healed enough to accept a beautiful love. A love that can withstand even the ravages of time. One that patiently and gently helps me remove my wall brick by brick. A love that feels like sunrise, breaking up the monotony of darkness. Because despite it all, real love is never a waste of time.

I won't love you like I loved him.
I can't love like that again.
Can't afford to lose myself,
In something that may end.
I won't trust you like I did him,
I can't be that naïve.
So forgive me when you tell the truth,
And it's hard for me to believe.
I won't need you like I did him.
Can't let myself fall hard.
Heartache always follows,
When I let down my guard.
So you see, I can't love you like I loved him.
I hope you understand.
But if you can be patient,
I can try to love again.

Love me deeply. Let your shadows dance with mine to the beat of our racing hearts. Love me at my best and even harder at my worst. Hold my hand without chaining my heart. Love me when I'm wilted and be amazed at how I return it once I bloom. So, love me deeply or leave me alone.

I see my hurt reflected in you almost like looking in a mirror. Our matching armor and skeptical glances as we peak from behind our guarded walls. It breaks my heart how badly I want to heal yours.

I don't want a spark; I want a slow burn.
I want a kiss that isn't a contract.
I don't want surface level; I want ocean depths.
I want to fall without being consumed.
I don't want for now; I want forever.

I say "my daughter" with so much pride that you'd think you belonged to me, but it is I who belongs to you. In a way I've never belonged to anyone else before. There is no part of you that wasn't once apart of me, yet my heart is so full of you that I can hardly call it my own anymore.

You are tethered to me for all eternity. Just as I am to my mother. Just as she is to hers. And so on. A legion of ancestral warrior women courses through your veins, cheering for your success. Even when I'm long gone, the invisible umbilical cord will connect us. I will always be with you.

You made him the sun.
Your world only lit up when he decided to shine upon you.
In the absence you ached for the chance to feel the light again.
You made him the sun but forgot that you are the moon.
Beautiful, mysterious, & strong enough to turn the tides.
Waxing and waning but ever present.
The moon has never played small to satisfy the sun.

I will love you so fiercely that you will question everyone that came before and anyone who comes after.

Love me fully,
Or just leave.
Either give me what I want,
Or give me what I need.

Know that you are the freshest air in my lungs. My heart living and walking outside of my body. You are my greatest accomplishment. Of all the great things my hands ever held, you are the best one by far. Know that I carry you in my heart no matter where I am. Know that even when I'm long gone, I will NEVER leave you. You are apart of me- the greatest parts of me. I will always be with you.

I don't want to consume you.
Nor do I want to be consumed.
I want to be whole, separately.
And come together to make something bigger than ourselves.

To say I fell in love with you would be a travesty of articulation. It would be more accurate to say I purposefully and recklessly left all inhibitions behind. I dove headfirst into the waters of your love. I willingly let the current of your affection wash over me until they cleansed away all relationship trauma and I was made new.

I want to sit with all the women I've been before. I want to hold them and tell them they aren't alone. That it gets better. I want to relive their pain from today's lens and offer them hope. To let them know that we are all together. The ghosts of every woman I've ever been rooting for me to win. The least I can do is hear them out.

I want to teach you that it's okay to take up space. That you don't have to apologize for existing in the world. Your skin, sexual orientation, body, or gender are not reasons you should ever have to apologize for. I want you to know that you have the right to be here without feeling like a burden. You've been given this gift of life and it's your right to unapologetically take up space. And in wanting these things for you I realized that I deserve the same grace. You've made me unafraid to take up space.

- Letters to my daughter

You spend your life knowing and learning to love your body and in an instant
it changes.
The home you once knew so intimately has changed over night.
Every part of this new body is foreign- like getting reacquainted to an old
friend all over again.
Some of us are just women relearning to love ourselves.

You're watching me. Learning confidence and how to love yourself from me. That is what makes me strive to promote a healthy body image regardless of my insecurities. How can I talk about all the things I perceive as flaws yet from the same mouth tell you how perfect you are and to always love yourself. Having a little girl made me a stronger woman. It forced me to do the soul work that I was avoiding.

Since when did it mean that being born a woman,
Meant cleaning up everyone's messes.
Since when did it mean that any bad that happens to you,
Was inadvertently caused by you?
Because apparently your choice in clothing can condemn you.
Since when was being too nice or not nice enough a death sentence?
Since when did everyone but you have autonomy over your body?
My dear, since forever.
Burdened is the one who bears the title "female."

Sometimes it's not a man.
Sometimes its laughing with your best friend until your stomach hurts.
Or laying on your mother's lap.
Or your heart beating to your child's drum.
-True love.

Are vessels named after the masculine?
Or planes? Land or sea?
No. Everything majestic is named in the feminine.
Remember that next time you doubt your greatness.

If heartache and suffering made the light in my eyes go out,
She set ablaze the largest forest.
She dragged the stars from the sky and let them camp outside my home.
She brought the light and gripped my heart,
Until she forced it to beat again.
\-   Ariyah

I know true love exists by the way my daughter looks at me like I put the stars in the sky.

In the very moment that I saw you, it took all of 1 second to soften the heart that time had hardened.

I've never seen him in the steepled buildings.
But I've seen him in the candy-colored sky at sunset.
I've seen him in a mother's strength.
In strangers who lend a helping hand.
In a child's innocence.
I've never seen God in church,
But I know he exists… because I've seen him.

There she is dancing.
Lighting up the room.
Dangerous enough to burn this place to the ground,
Yet kind enough to provide warmth.
To mistake her kindness for weakness is foolish.

Blindly putting one foot in front of the other
Trusting that the path to where I'm going will appear.
-faith

I was born to dance under the stars and giggle with my friends. To love and be loved deeply by all I allow into my space. I was born to run freely and untamed. My chaos is beautiful and my wild can feel like home. I was born an imperfect goddess.

My heart is the people's champ. It's black and blue from all its's been through but me and my bruised heart always come out on top in the end.

RESOURCES

With mental health being such a prevalent issue in the world today, it was really important to me to make sure this book included resources for anyone struggling. I see you, and you are not alone.

Mental Health

Crisis Hot line- 988
Local Emergency- 911
Text "HOME" to 741741
Online Chat: 988Lifeline.org/chat
Veterans Text- 838255

Addiction

National Helpline- 1.800.622.HELP (4357)
Text your zip code to 435748

Sexual Assault

National Hot line- 1.800.656.4673
Veterans & Dependent Hot line- 877.995.5247

Domestic Violence

Hot line- 800.799.SAFE or 866.331.9474

The acronym "ACCEPTS" outlines seven techniques to distract yourself from distressing thoughts until they pass.

ACTIVITIES
Do an activity that requires concentration (reading, writing, move your body, etc.)

CONTRIBUTING
Do something for someone else (volunteer, make a gift, etc.)

COMPARISONS
Put your situation into perspective by comparing a worse experience

EMOTIONS
Put your situation into perspective by comparing a worse experience

PUSHING AWAY
Block it from your mind by using imagery (Imagine your happy place)

THOUGHTS
Shift your thoughts to something neutral

SENSATIONS
Find safe physical sensations to distract you (Focus on smell, taste, touch, hear)

ABOUT THE AUTHOR

In the rich tapestry of life, Bree Sprual emerges as a proud veteran, a devoted single mother, and a self proclaimed, "girl's girl." Drawing from the depths of her own struggles, Bree crafts pieces that resonate with raw emotion and unwavering honesty. Each verse reflects her own journey, woven with threads of hope, empathy, and an unwavering belief in the power of resilience. Through her words, she endeavors to create a safe haven where women can find solace, strength, and solidarity. Bree is not just a poet; she is a compassionate voice in the realm of mental health advocacy, uplifting and empowering women to embrace their strength and resilience. Together, they are warriors, traversing life's battlefield with grace, courage, and the unshakeable belief that they are stronger together.

www.ingramcontent.com/pod-product-compliance
Lightning Source LLC
Chambersburg PA
CBHW051329120626
46547CB00016B/2466